THE COOLEST JOBS ON THE PLANET

polar scientist

Emily Shuckburgh with Catherine Chambers

Raintree

Chicago, Illinois

Edited by Andrew Farrow, Christine Peterson, and
Helen Cox Cannons
Designed by Cynthia Akiyoshi
Original illustrations © Capstone Global Library Limited 2014
Illustrated by HL Studios
Picture research by Mica Brancic and Tracy Cummins
Production by Helen McCreath
Originated by Capstone Global Library Limited
Printed and bound in China by CTPS

18 17 16 15 14
10 9 8 7 6 5 4 3 2 1

Library of Congress Cataloging-in-Publication Data
Shuckburgh, Emily, author.
    Polar scientist : the coolest jobs on the planet / Emily Shuckburgh
with Catherine Chambers.
        pages cm. — (The coolest jobs on the planet)
Includes bibliographical references and index.
    ISBN 978-1-4109-6642-1 (hb) — ISBN 978-1-4109-6648-3
(pb) 1. Climatology — Vocational guidance — Juvenile literature.
2. Shuckburgh, Emily — Juvenile literature. 3. Climatologists —
Biography — Juvenile literature. 4. Women scientists — Biography —
Juvenile literature. I. Chambers, Catherine, 1954- author. II. Title.

QC869.5.S58 2015
551.6023 — dc23   2013040701

Acknowledgments
We would like to thank the following for permission to reproduce
photographs: Alamy pp. 40-41 (© Rice Jackson); BAS pp. 4, 5,
26, 27, 28, 32, 33, 34, 35 (all Emily Shuckburgh), 11 (Agnieszka
Fryckowska), 14 & 38 top (both Chris Gilbert), 19 (Bryn Jones),
20 (Teal Riley), 21 (Catherine Moore), 6, 22, 25, 37 & 38 bottom
(all Pete Bucktrout), 23 (Sam Burrell), 36 (Roger Stilwell), 39
(Morag Hunter); Corbis Reuters/Alister Doyle p. 7; FLPA p. 15
(ImageBroker/Imagebroker); Getty Images pp. 18 (Popperfoto/
Captain Robert Falcon Scott), 31 (The Image Bank/Ken Graham);
NASA pp. 10, 13; Naturepl.com p.8 (Ben Osborne); NOC
Southampton pp. 24 (Andy Webb), 29 (Katy Sheen), San Diego
Supercomputer Center, UC San Diego p. 16 (Matt Mazloff); Science
Photo Library p. 17 (Dee Breger), Shutterstock pp. 42 boots
(Aptyp_koK), 42 coffee (magicoven), 42 cookie (Sergio33), 42
hand (DenisNata), 42 wind vane (Gwoeii); SuperStock p. 9 (Juice
Images). Design elements Shutterstock.

Cover photo of the *James Clark Ross* reproduced with permission of
BAS/Pete Bucktrout.

007008CTPSF14

contents

The Magic Moment

I'M EMILY SHUCKBURGH, head of the Open Oceans research group at the British Antarctic Survey (BAS). It's chilly here on Antarctica's Southern Ocean, but the science is exciting!

My amazing magic moment happened back in the year 2000. It was my first time as a member of a science team in the Arctic.

We were releasing science research balloons into the atmosphere. As the balloons rose, they dazzled in the sunlight, and the wispy clouds around them shimmered with all the colors of the rainbow above the snowy landscape. It was spectacular.

We sent the balloons up to investigate the destruction of the ozone layer, which creates an invisible filter that acts like a protective sunscreen around Earth. It shields Earth from the Sun's harmful ultraviolet (UV) rays that can burn our skin. In recent decades, the layer has thinned.

Did you know?

The clouds I saw were made of frozen crystals, which only form in polar winter temperatures of below −108 degrees Fahrenheit (−78 degrees Celsius). Sunlight shining through the crystals makes rainbow colors. Chemical changes occur on the surface of these crystals, releasing chlorine from the gases (CFCs) once used in aerosol cans and refrigerators. In the spring, the stronger sunlight acts on the chlorine in the atmosphere, destroying the protective ozone layer around Earth.

NOTE TO SELF

The work I do tries to shed light on environmental change and its effects on the planet. This science needs a lot of math, and I'm a trained mathematician. Could there be any better way to use my skills?

THE IMPORTANCE OF ANTARCTICA

My research is on climate change and focuses on Antarctica's Southern Ocean and the atmosphere above it. We are trying to find out how climate change affects Antarctica, and how changes there affect the rest of the planet. This ocean is a special place to research, because it actually helps the world to slow climate change. We need this help because Earth's climate is getting warmer.

We monitor the atmosphere, ocean, sea ice, and ice sheets for changes.

Normally, the Sun warms Earth, and carbon gases form a blanket that traps heat around our planet. This is the natural greenhouse effect. But humans burn a lot of fossil fuels, such as coal, oil, and gas, releasing extra carbon gases into the atmosphere. These form a thicker blanket that traps more heat around Earth, causing our climate to change.

The Southern Ocean helps us by soaking up about 10 percent of the carbon dioxide humans put into the atmosphere each year. This slows climate change. But how long can the ocean keep absorbing carbon? Finding answers is my voyage of discovery.

In March 2008, the Wilkins Ice Shelf on the rapidly warming Antarctic Peninsula suddenly collapsed. It lost more than 160 square miles (400 square kilometers) of its ice.

65 feet

Did you know?

Antarctica's ice sheet is the largest ice mass on Earth. In summer, there is less ice, and it still covers almost 5.4 million square miles (14 million square kilometers). This ice reflects about 80 percent of the Sun's rays, helping to keep Earth cool.

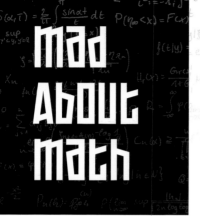

mad about math

I need to use a lot of math to do my work, and it was math that brought me to polar science. In school, I found problem-solving and mathematical patterns really fascinating. But I also loved being in the countryside, identifying and learning the names of wild flowers. So mathematics, nature, and patterns were early interests that propelled me toward the job I do now.

Growing up, I was glued to television documentaries such as David Attenborough's *Life in the Freezer* (above). These amazing programs show the richness of Antarctica's wildlife. It took 20 team members and 3 years in very icy, stormy conditions to film them.

Kids enjoy science and math classes like this one, which show how these skills can be applied to the real world.

In the 1980s, I also tuned in to a weekly science and technology television series called *Tomorrow's World*. Programs like this showed an increasing amount of research into the growth of ozone holes and environmental change. I was inspired to become a scientist myself!

MY HERO!
Judith Hann
(born 1942)

Judith hosted *Tomorrow's World* between 1974 and 1994. Judith is a zoologist— an animal expert—but is passionate about many fields of science and the environment.

NOTE TO SELF

I often think of the great time I had in the advanced math classes I took as a kid during my free time on Saturdays. The classes showed math in the real world. At last, I had real-life problems to solve. I saw the possibilities of math—and the fun!

I went on to study math in college. Afterward, I began to use my math skills in weather forecasting and climate change. It helped me to set up my own weather company. I wanted to help people plan their businesses and lives.

Math can explain the swirling cloud patterns seen in this satellite image. Here, they have been formed as the wind has hit Jan Mayen Island in the Greenland Sea.

WEATHER AND CLIMATE

Weather is what we experience over a short period, such as a week, while climate occurs over a long period, such as 30 years. I use math to forecast tomorrow's weather by putting today's weather data, including temperature and air pressure, into a computer simulation. It can be quite difficult to predict weather, because even slight changes in data can make a huge difference in the forecast.

A scientist launches a weather balloon. This carries a small package of instruments that measure temperature, pressure, and humidity up to a height of 15 miles (25 kilometers). Launches occur every day throughout the year.

I use a similar computer simulation to predict the climate, but I need to input data on the amount of carbon dioxide in the atmosphere. I am particularly interested in the patterns of winds and ocean currents and how they change over time. Swirling patterns known as eddies form storm systems in the atmosphere and are also found in the ocean.

Did you know?

Scientists study how tiny changes at the beginning of a system, such as the weather, can have a big impact. We call this impact chaos theory. It also teaches us that nature works in patterns, and patterns are what my work is all about.

TOOLS OF THE TRADE: WEATHER BALLOONS

Weather balloons carry bundles of instruments called radiosondes, which contain sensors that measure temperature, atmospheric pressure, wind, and humidity. Instruments called transponders send the data back to computers on Earth. High-rising weather balloons won't pop easily, because they are made of a material that can resist pressure way up in the atmosphere.

POLES

After I received a higher college degree called a doctorate, I continued studies that led me in the year 2000 to the Arctic, and to my magic moment (see pages 4–5). The use of chlorofluorocarbons (CFCs) that thin out the ozone layer had been banned in 1989, in an international treaty called the Montreal Protocol. But old CFCs are still very active in the atmosphere.

Did you know?

The Arctic and the Antarctic are both frozen worlds, but in many ways they are poles apart! The North Pole is in the Arctic, and the South Pole is in the Antarctic. The Arctic is an ocean surrounded by an icy continent, but the Antarctic is an icy continent surrounded by ocean. The Arctic tern travels each year from its Arctic breeding grounds to its wintering grounds off Antarctica, covering some 25,000 miles (40,000 kilometers)! This is the farthest yearly journey of any bird.

MY HERO!
Joseph Farman
(1930–2013)

On my first field trip, I met the incredible Professor Joseph Farman. Every year since 1956, he'd measured ozone levels in the atmosphere above Antarctica. In 1985, Joe alerted a disbelieving world to the ozone "holes."

MY HERO!
Susan Solomon
(born 1956)

I was inspired to study polar science by Susan Solomon. She is an expert on the chemistry of the ozone hole and on climate change and has led science expeditions to Antarctica. She also wrote a book about the weather conditions on Captain Robert Falcon Scott's fatal South Pole expedition (see page 18).

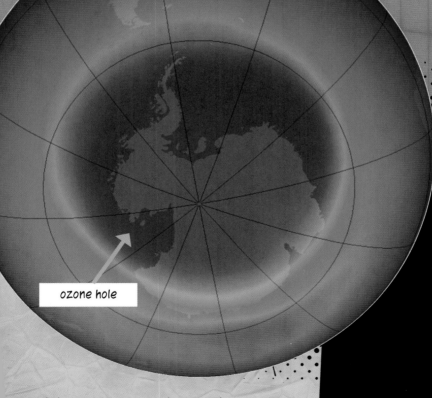

ozone hole

This NASA satellite image over Antarctica's ozone hole was taken in 2012, during September, a month when ozone is thin. It is shown by the blue and purple colors.

MEASURING OZONE LEVELS
MEASURING OZONE LEVELS
MEASURING OZONE LEVELS

MEASURING OZONE LEVELS

I learned a lot from the way Joe Farman (see page 12) did his science. Joe had measured ozone levels in Antarctica every year with old Dobson spectrometers, instruments invented in 1924. He was passionate about patient, hands-on data collecting. In my own science, I often use computer models, but I also test them with real experiments in Antarctica's icy waters.

Joe (left) and his team were so astounded by the low ozone readings that they ordered new Dobson spectrometers to double-check them. These recorded even lower levels!

Polar bears now find it difficult to feed in summer on ice floes in some parts of Hudson Bay because many have melted. Their habitat is being altered by climate change.

I like to keep in touch with how climate change affects people and the environment. So, on my first field trips to Canada's Arctic region, I talked to some locals. They told me that in the past, every December, they sledded across the ice on Hudson Bay from their village to the main town, Iqaluit. But for many years now the ice has been too thin. Is this due to climate change? It's my job to find out.

TOOLS OF THE TRADE: SATELLITE IMAGES

We use satellite images and data to measure ice and snow melt. The Arctic Sea ice melts over the summer, reaching its minimum extent in September each year. But this is now just half what it was 30 years ago.

ANSWERS IN THE POLAR OCEAN

I was now sure that I wanted to find some answers to climate change in the motion of the Southern Ocean and the atmosphere above it. So I took up research posts, working with great scientists in France and the United States.

In 2009, I became in charge of Open Oceans for the British Antarctic Survey. This means my working life is now dedicated to the poles. There, I focus on the circulation and global influence of the Arctic Ocean, and the Southern Ocean around Antarctica.

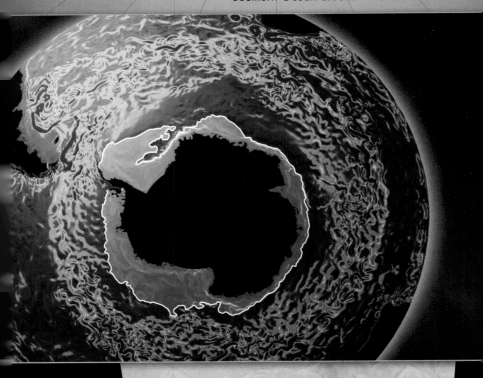

This is Antarctic Circumpolar Current (ACC) in the Southern Ocean. Slow-moving currents are shown in blue and fast-moving currents are in red. The volume of its waters is the same as 500 Amazon Rivers! Any change occurring in the ACC affects the Atlantic, Pacific, and Indian Ocean systems connected to it.

We're especially interested in eddies, which are like atmospheric storms, but in the oceans. These pools of swirling, churning waters, blown by fierce winds, can change the oceans' circulation. This can affect the way old carbon layers from the seabed are churned up, and how much carbon the ocean absorbs from the atmosphere.

Satellite images capture huge swirling areas of tiny sea plants called phytoplankton, which show how a current is moving. They absorb carbon dioxide, which they need to grow. They are thus a good indicator of carbon levels in the sea.

Did you know?

The world's coal, oil, and gas reserves contain about 500 billion tonnes of carbon, which can be released into the atmosphere when we burn it for fuel. But there are a massive 6 trillion tonnes of it lying at the bottom of our oceans in marine sediments.

Preparing for Antarctica

Field trips to the Arctic prepared me a little for my first expedition to Antarctica. But only a little! Because Antarctica is the chilliest, windiest continent on Earth. In winter, temperatures can drop to –78 degrees Fahrenheit (–60 degrees Celsius). Howling winds can speed along at over 100 miles (160 kilometers) per hour. And with whipped-up snow and ice, it can be really hard to see. The summer months, when I go, are a bit warmer, although the wind can still blow hard.

MY HERO!

Captain Robert Falcon Scott (1868–1912)

Captain Robert Falcon Scott is most famous for his heroic 1912 expedition to the South Pole, where he died with his team (above) on the Ross Ice Shelf. But I admire him also for his serious scientific aims, choosing a team that gave us so much knowledge of Antarctica's climate, geology, flora, fauna, magnetism, and fossils.

On our polar science vessel in the Southern Ocean, even faster winds can churn up colossal 40-foot (12-meter) waves, even in summer. We can't do science when conditions are like this. Even when it's calmer, we find the icy cold difficult to cope with sometimes. And seasickness can be a problem for some of the team members.

Did you know?

Most of my field science takes place in summer, because the seas freeze over in winter. But marine biologists go in winter to study life under the ice. They also observe the effects of global temperature changes on the lives of Antarctica's amazing creatures, such as the Emperor penguin.

It's no surprise that before we go, we have to learn about Antarctic conditions. We also take part in a week-long, very intensive training course.

As part of the training, we practice sea survival in a pool designed to copy many different sea conditions. We're thrown into the "ocean" in really scary fake storms. We practice jumping onto a life raft from a tall height, too. It's serious stuff, but really cool.

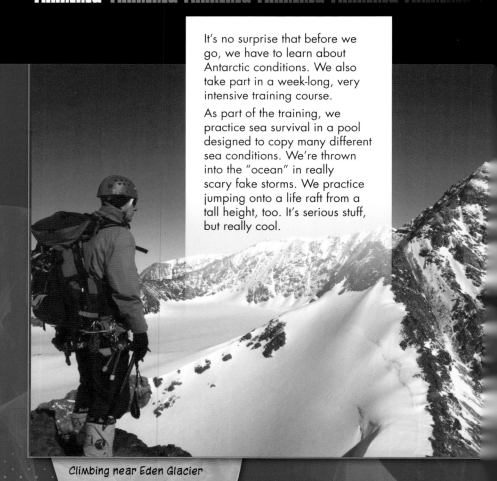

Climbing near Eden Glacier

TOOLS OF THE TRADE: TOOLS FOR CLIMBING MOUNTAINS

Some science takes place up Antarctica's icy mountains. To climb them, we need ice axes, ice screws, and crampons over our boots to help grip the ice. The brittle ice is formed from snow that compacted over countless years. Newer snow is fragile, so snow anchors are needed. These are metal bars buried deep, with ropes attached to them.

This is Drake Passage, where I work on the Southern Ocean. When this picture was taken, there was a Force 12 gale, and I couldn't do my experiments in that!

NOTE TO SELF

First-aid skills are hugely important. We're trained to cope with human casualties by practicing on professional actors. They're scarily good at pretending to roll around in pain with severe injuries. There's a lot of fake blood, too!

WELL DRESSED AND WELL FED

Our bodies can never adjust to extreme cold, so we learn how to dress for it. Light layers are best because they trap air, which is warmed by our body's heat. The first is the "wicking layer." This draws sweat away from the skin into outer layers, where it evaporates. It's really important to keep dry.

I'm wearing a hat because you lose 20 percent of body heat from your head. The wrists, ankles, and neck are also heat-loss hot spots.

NOTE TO SELF

Hypothermia is a life-threatening dip in body temperature. Normal body temperature is 98.6 degrees Fahrenheit (37 degrees Celsius), and hypothermia starts when it falls below 95 degrees Fahrenheit (35 degrees Celsius) — that's not much of a drop. First you shiver, then blood flow slows in your fingers and toes and you start to feel dizzy.

In winter, it is dark all day long at the Halley Research Station, with the only light coming from the aurora in the sky. There are no deliveries of fresh food in winter!

Did you know?

Pemmican is an ancient recipe of concentrated fat and dried meat protein — one of the first high-energy bars. Pemmican was developed by North American Arctic peoples and was often made of moose, bison, or elk. Captain Scott (see page 18) used it, and you can still buy commercially made bars today.

THE RRS *JAMES CLARK ROSS*

Now I'm ready to join the RRS *James Clark Ross,* the science ship that will be my home and my workplace for many weeks to come. Welcome aboard! The *James Clark Ross* is a floating laboratory where scientists examine seawater and biological specimens. It's where a whole host of data about the ocean is collected.

The *James Clark Ross* has many special features to cope with icy conditions and to assist scientific experiments. The ship can be steered very slowly through flat sea ice that is 3.3 feet (1 meter) thick and rolls slightly, so that the ice does not squeeze the hull.

It has been designed to move quietly so that underwater acoustic equipment can deliver accurate results.

This is an Autonomous Underwater Vehicle. We can now send ones like this beneath the ice to take measurements of the ocean underneath.

Did you know?

Our ship was named after Rear-Admiral James Clark Ross (1800–1862). He discovered the magnetic North Pole in 1931. During 1840–43, he made three scientific voyages to the Southern Ocean, where he discovered the Ross Sea and Victoria Land, with its snow-covered mountains and ribbons of glaciers.

While the waters of the Southern Ocean are my main focus, there are many other projects that we can do from the ship. One of these is measuring the thickness of the ice over a period of time. This can tell us how much heat is lost from the ocean to the atmosphere—a process that affects climate.

TOOLS OF THE TRADE: ICE MASS BALANCE BUOYS

You can see from the picture that the RRS *James Clark Ross* is off-loading ice-mass balance buoys to measure ice thickness. Among other instruments, these buoys carry digital chips that record temperature, and some even have webcams.

SECRETS IN THE SEA

We take water samples in the Southern Ocean to see its temperature and how salty it is. This can tell us where the water has come from. We can detect surprisingly warm, salty water that came from the North Atlantic and traveled south in the ocean circulation. Our measurements look for changes over time in this circulation. We also take measurements to help us understand how the Southern Ocean influences the climate across Earth.

But it's not just our climate that depends on the chilly waters around Antarctica. Amazingly, the Southern Ocean supplies nutrients that fertilize 75 percent of plant and animal growth in the rest of the world's oceans!

NOTE TO SELF

One of the great things about working in Antarctica is that I know there are teams from 30 nations here. There's often cooperation between us — for example, the U.S. National Science Foundation and the British Antarctic Survey worked together on a high altitude balloon campaign to collect data from the atmosphere.

Here we are lowering a circular frame into the water with 24 Niskin bottles that we can open and close at different depths to take water samples.

Here we are emptying the Niskin bottles to analyze the water in the laboratory on the ship. We measure the amount of salt and other chemicals.

MY HERO!

Captain Robert Fitzroy
(1805–1865)

Captain Robert Fitzroy sailed the *Beagle* to the edge of the Southern Ocean with the famous scientist Charles Darwin onboard. Using navigation charts, thermometers, barometers, and excellent record keeping, Fitzroy became the world's first weather forecaster, and he made meteorology a recognized science.

Before I tell you about the challenges of everyday life in Antarctica, I'll explain one of our current projects.

At Last! An Expedition!

It's all about eddies and what they can tell us about changes in ocean currents and climate patterns. Satellite data can give us some information. But to really understand the details, we have to take direct measurements from the Southern Ocean. We've been using two methods.

The first is when we release a chemical dye in the ocean. This tracks the ocean flow and can tell us how the eddies and the strong winds that blow over the Southern Ocean affect the circulation. We're also interested in how the dye is stirred and mixed as the ocean flows over the seabed.

Here I am about to set off from the Falkland Islands on our ship the RRS James Clark Ross.

I'm most interested in the second method of taking measurements from the Southern Ocean. To do this, we drop floats down into the water and follow their course as they bob around like rubber ducks in the ocean currents. We use these floats to trace out the patterns of mixing created by the eddies.

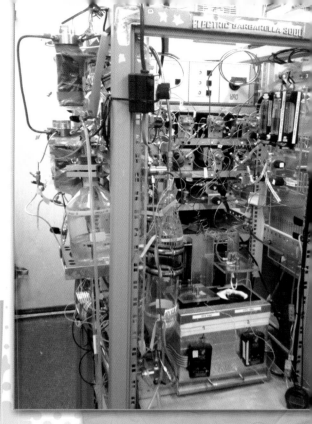

This equipment detects the concentration of dye in seawater.

Did you know?

One of the floats we released near Drake Passage at the tip of South America made it all the way across the Atlantic to South Africa 18 months later!

TOOLS OF THE TRADE: ROBOTIC FLOATS

There are more than 3,000 robotic floats in the world's oceans! Some drift at the sea surface, while others are deep-diving, taking measurements of temperature and saltiness. These transmit their data back via satellites when they reach the surface. Some are tracked acoustically while they're underwater. That means they're traced by using equipment that bounces sound off them.

USING ECHOSOUNDERS

Now we're on the Southern Ocean, buffeted by wind and waves. Here, the Circumpolar Current rushes through the narrow point at Drake Passage between Antarctica and South America, swirling with eddies as it goes.

Unlocking the secrets of our oceans' currents involves other areas of research, such as measuring the seabed's hills and valleys over which the sea passes. A huge instrument called an echosounder collects the measurements. The data is then used to create maps.

TOOLS OF THE TRADE: ECHOSOUNDER

From the ship's hull, an echosounder sends out beams of sound that hit the seabed, then return to a transducer, which measures the journey time for each hit. A short journey time, for example, means that the seabed at that point rises close to the surface.

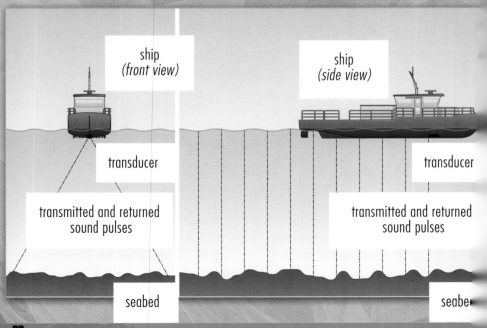

ship
(front view)

ship
(side view)

transducer

transducer

transmitted and returned
sound pulses

transmitted and returned
sound pulses

seabed

seabe

We also need to know the chemical makeup of Antarctica's seawater. In our onboard laboratories, the sea's acidity is measured. This is because when the ocean absorbs more carbon, it becomes more acidic. In January 2013, the BAS led a team of 30 scientists to test for acidity and its effects on marine life, such as dissolving sea-snail shells.

Did you know?

International treaties are, for the moment, protecting Antarctica from oil exploration and mining, unlike in the Arctic. Climate change is melting the sea ice in the Arctic, opening it up to transit by ships and allowing oil and mining companies to tap into previously untapped reserves.

The Arctic holds about 30 percent of the planet's untapped natural gas reserves and 13 percent of its oil.

A Day in the Life

It's another thrilling day on the RRS *James Clark Ross*. Will the weather allow us to follow our packed science schedule? I can relax a little, knowing that I'm part of a great team of scientists. Our expeditions usually last at least six weeks, so teamwork is essential.

Here I am with my team from the night shift!

My "working day" is often my "working night"! We operate 24-hour days, so the ship and the science never sleep. Each of us sticks to the same shift on an expedition. So it could be from 8:00 a.m. to 4:00 p.m.; from 4:00 p.m. to midnight; or from midnight to 8:00 a.m. Sometimes these 8-hour shifts extend to 12 hours so that we can complete the day's work.

The floats are packaged inside boxes. We give each float a name—here's one called Emily!

I GOT THE NIGHT SHIFT!

It's 8:00 a.m. I've just finished the night shift, but there's a team meeting before I can eat and get some rest. Our chief scientist sets the goals, and the ship's captain tells us if it's safe to go ahead with them.

TOOLS OF THE TRADE: DROGUED FLOATS

Last night we were setting floats into the water at points where satellite information pointed to eddies. The floats are spherical, with a drogue parachute attached to each. This parachute stabilizes the float and makes sure that ocean currents, not the wind, are moving it.

After the meeting, I enjoy my dinner— the chefs cook some great meals! I go to bed, but the rolling waves make sleep difficult.

After an early evening "breakfast," I write up notes on our experiments and then go on deck for the day's task. This time we're pulling in devices called a CDT (Conductivity, Depth, and Temperature) and a VMP (Vertical Microstructure Profiler). CDTs take important measurements of chemicals in the ocean. VMPs help tell us where the ocean's mixing occurs.

But the VMP has been lost! The wind's whipping up the waves and we're blowing off course, so locating it is not an easy task. It's summertime in Antarctica, so daylight lasts almost all night long. It's hard to spot the light on the VMP, but finally its flag is sighted!

Flocks of birds help us locate our VMPs! And shoals of fish, whales, and dolphins also seem to be really curious about our instruments!

VMP

After a quick lunch, the crew uses cables to haul up the CDT frame. We remove the bottles and take them to the onboard laboratory for analysis.

I'm testing samples for carbon gases using a dangerous chemical called mercuric chloride. So, I have to wear a special outfit and protective goggles.

science on ice

Sometimes I visit our research stations on land. Or I should say, on ice! Because about 96 percent of Antarctica is covered with snow and ice all year round.

The tiny 4 percent left is mainly bare rock with a little vegetation—some mosses, lichens, a little grass, and just two species of flower. However, this area of vegetation is larger than it was, which is possibly another sign of climate change.

Did you know?

We're trying hard to develop environmentally friendly technology to run our stations. Our waste is shipped far away from Antarctica for disposal. On one trip, our ship stopped at Damoy Point to dig out and remove two old broken snowmobiles. We all really need to pitch in!

This is Rothera Research Station,
built on the Antarctic Peninsula's
Adelaide Island.

My work takes me to Rothera Research
Station, which is a large complex that
includes science laboratories, offices,
workshops, a hangar for aircraft, a landing
stage for ships, and an operations control
tower. We even get to relax in a recreation
area. Things have moved on since Joe
Farman's day. He had to melt snow just to
make a cup of tea!

NOTE TO SELF

I like linking up with other
scientists, whose work adds to the
big picture. For example, we can
now track how species adapted to
climate change in the past through
DNA testing. Certain species are
monitored every year to find out if
current climate change is affecting
their populations.

Getting around on a snowmobile is fun! It also allows me to see field science research, such as ice-core sampling. In recent years, ice cores have given us an amazing window into climate change going back 800,000 years. Ice cores show us that current carbon gas levels are higher than at any other time since then. For my projects, they reveal previous cycles of ice age freezing and melting, and how the amount of carbon stored in the Southern Ocean changes as the temperature changes.

Above, some scientists drill down and get samples of ice core. As layer after layer of snow builds up, tiny bubbles of air are trapped in the ice. You can see those bubbles in this slice of ice core (right).

NOTE TO SELF

Antarctica holds so many surprises, such as carbon gas bubbles that pop from melting ice cores. If I get close enough to the bubbles, I can breathe in air that's hundreds of thousands of years old. This is from a time when the earliest forms of humankind had only just started gathering around campfires. Amazing!

We couldn't get by without our light aircraft. In addition to mapping Antarctica and other activities, they also take us home. Our Twin Otter aircraft take off on skis rather than wheels along an icy glacier strip (see below).

Did you know?

Antarctica has ice that is up to 2.9 miles (4.7 kilometers) thick. This ice preserves a record of climate conditions exactly at the time it was frozen. It gives us the amounts of gases in the atmosphere and the temperature at that time.

Looking Ahead

I hope you can now see that the poles are really special places, where stunning scenery and wildlife are matched by amazing scientific phenomena on both sea and land. They are places where nature gives us so many clues to climate change. We just have to work hard at finding the answers.

NOTE TO SELF

By the way, I never forgot who inspired me to follow my dreams as a mathematician and scientist. In 1999, I joined the *Tomorrow's World* team (see page 9), hopefully encouraging young mathematicians to become polar scientists, too.

I never forget how amazing the sights of Antarctica are, like this ice formation in Pleneau Bay.

I'm passionate about communicating our scientific discoveries to many different groups, from politicians to leaders of industry. Studying the atmosphere, oceans, and ice at the poles has helped us conclude that humans are disrupting the climate by putting carbon dioxide into the atmosphere.

Unless we find alternatives, the climate will be disrupted further, with substantial changes not just at the poles, but across the world. Will human creativity solve this problem? It is up to each and every one of us to do our part!

Did you know?

In 2013, top scientists from around the world confirmed human-made climate change in a report by the Intergovernmental Panel on Climate Change (IPCC). The report makes some environmental predictions for the future. One of these is that sea levels could rise by about 1.5 to 3 feet (0.5 to 1 meters) by the end of the century if we continue to put carbon dioxide into the atmosphere as we do now.

QUIZ

Do you have what it takes to become a polar scientist?

1. It's winter and there's snow on the ground. Do you...

a) Stay indoors, shivering under a blanket?

b) Run straight outside and play in the freezing cold?

c) Put on warm clothes, boots, and a hat, then go outside?

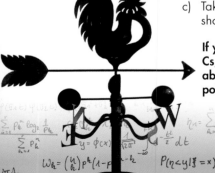

2. You are taken to a science and technology museum. Which of these do you do?

a) Look quickly at the exhibits and then find a snack.

b) Head straight for the cafeteria and stay there.

c) Look carefully at all the exhibits and take part in the interactive ones.

3. You make a weather vane at school. You are then asked to take it home and record the direction of the wind every day on your two-week vacation. Do you...

a) Take measurements, but only for the first week?

b) Forget to set up the weather vane?

c) Take measurements every day and create a chart showing the results?

If you answered mostly Cs, you should think about becoming a polar scientist!

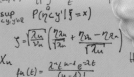

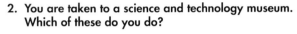

42

How much can you remember about what you have read in this book?

1. Which type of gases destroy ozone in the atmosphere?

2. What type of gas increases climate change?

3. How fast can the wind blow in Antarctica?

4. True or false? Humans put carbon dioxide into the atmosphere by burning fossil fuels such as gas, coal, and oil.

5. Unscramble these letters to spell the name of an instrument that measures the thickness of the ozone layer from the ground. Hint: There are two words.

    ctseordeompbnosret

6. True or false? The thinning of the ozone layer is the major cause of global warming.

7. How thick can the ice in Antarctica measure at its deepest point?

Glossary

air pressure force of air above us down on Earth. Air pressure measurements help predict weather.

atmosphere layers of gases high above Earth

carbon dioxide one of the carbon gases that are also called greenhouse gases

chaos theory idea that tiny changes within a system can have a big impact on the system as a whole, such as a weather system

chlorofluorocarbon (CFC) gas that destroys the protective ozone layer in the atmosphere around Earth

climate typical weather that occurs over a long period of time

computer simulation computer program that represents something in the real world

crampon spiky metal frame around a climbing shoe to help climbers grip ice

drogue parachute parachute attached to a science float. It makes sure that ocean currents are moving the float, not the wind.

eddy like a storm in the atmosphere, but occurring in the oceans

fauna animal life

flora plant life

geology study of Earth's rock structure

hypothermia when the body becomes dangerously cold and starts to shut down

ice core very long tube of ice dug out of huge ice sheets. Ice cores tell us a lot about past climate change.

lichen small, plant-like organism. It is a mixture of plant parts and fungus parts.

magnetism force between objects producing areas around them that attract or push away other objects. Magnetism is strongest at the poles.

meteorology study of the processes and behavior of the atmosphere, usually to forecast the weather

nutrient food

ozone invisible layer of gases that surround Earth, protecting it from the Sun, a bit like sunscreen

pemmican food with high fat and dried protein in it. It is eaten in cold climates to provide energy.

phytoplankton tiny sea plants that start Earth's food chain

radiosonde bundle of instruments that measure weather data in the atmosphere. They are attached to high-rising weather balloons.

sediment rocks and soils washed down from the land to the seabed or riverbed

snow anchor strong metal bar buried deep in snow with a rope attached to help climbers in snowy conditions

snowmobile open motorized vehicle designed to ride over snow and ice

ultraviolet (UV) invisible wavelengths of light that come from the Sun. Too many UV rays reaching Earth can burn people's skin.

weather conditions such as temperature, wind, sunshine, and rain

Find out more

BOOKS

Bledsoe, Lucy Jane. *How to Survive in Antarctica*. New York: Holiday House, 2006.

Green, Jen. *Frozen Extremes* (Extreme Nature). New York: Crabtree, 2009.

Hunter, Rebecca. *Climate Change* (Eco Alert). Mankato, Minn.: Sea-to-Sea, 2012.

Parker, Steve. *100 Facts: Polar Lands*. Broomall, Pa.: MC, 2010.

Royston, Angela. *Climate Change* (Headline Issues). Chicago: Heinemann Library, 2009.

Woodward, John. *Climate Change* (Eyewitness). New York: Dorling Kindersley, 2008.

WEB SITES

www.antarctica.ac.uk/staff-profiles/webspace/emsh/bio.html
For more about Emily's work, see her British Antarctic Survey web page.

climatekids.nasa.gov/polar-temperatures
Find out more about the poles.

www.epa.gov/sunwise/kids/kids_ozone.html
This web site includes information about the ozone layer.

ngm.nationalgeographic.com/ngm/antarctica/
This National Geographic site features an interactive map with lots of information about Antarctica.

video.nationalgeographic.com/video/environment/global-warming-environment/antarctica-ice/
This National Geographic video explores the effects of climate change in Antarctica.

www.worldatlas.com/webimage/countrys/an.htm
Learn more about Antarctica on this web site.

PLACES TO VISIT

Exploratorium
Pier 15
San Francisco, California 94111
www.exploratorium.edu
A visit to the Exploratorium could help you learn all about the science principles that Emily mentions in this book.

Smithsonian National Museum of Natural History
10th Street and Constitution Avenue NW
Washington, D.C. 20560
www.mnh.si.edu
This is another great museum where you can explore science.

Index